Child of the Silent Night

YEARLING BOOKS are designed especially to entertain and enlighten young people. Charles F. Reasoner, Professor Emeritus of Children's Literature and Reading, New York University, is consultant to this series.

For a complete listing of all Yearling titles, write to Dell Publishing Co., Inc., Promotion Department, P.O. Box 3000, Pine Brook, N.J. 07058.

EDITH FISHER HUNTER

Child of the Silent Night

Illustrated by Bea Holmes

A YEARLING BOOK

Published by
Dell Publishing Co., Inc.
1 Dag Hammarskjold Plaza
New York, New York 10017

To Frances Way Fisher,
who first introduced me to
the story of Laura Bridgman

Yearling ® TM 913705, Dell Publishing Co., Inc.

ISBN: 0-440-71223-8

Reprinted by arrangement with Houghton Mifflin Company
Printed in the United States of America
Book Club Edition
Previous Dell edition #41223-4
One printing
New Dell edition
First printing—January 1984

A LITTLE GIRL was sitting on a granite rock that extended out over a rushing brook. Her legs dangled down near the water and in her hand she held a long stick. The other end of the stick was deep in the water.

The little girl's name was Laura. On this warm day in early May the brook was so swelled with melted snow that it was almost a river. The swirling water seemed to be trying to pull the stick right out of Laura's hand. She clutched it with all her might. She was not going to let go of it. She would let the brook pull her in before she would let go!

Beside Laura sat Uncle Asa Tenney. He had tight hold of her arm. He knew that although

Laura was seven years old she was not as strong as most seven-year-olds. She certainly was not as strong as a swollen stream in early May in New Hampshire. He had no intention of letting Laura follow her stick into the water.

Laura was wondering as she and Uncle Asa sat there by the brook. She could remember the last time they had taken the walk that brought them here. It had been an icy cold day. There had been some snow still on the ground and they had worn boots and warm coats. Most amazing of all, they had been able to walk on the brook!

Laura wondered how that could possibly be. How could people walk on brooks when it was very cold but when it was warm they must be careful not to fall into them? In cold weather, she wondered to herself, does the brook have a cover like the well at home?

Her mother and father never let her go near the well unless the cover was on. But the cover

of the well was not slippery like the cover of the brook. She remembered sliding on the brook with Uncle Asa. She would have to think some more about all this.

At last Laura took her stick out of the brook. She was satisfied that she had won the tug-of-war. She laid the stick on the rock beside her, and felt about until she found a stone to throw into the water. The stone felt smooth. She rubbed it against her cheek.

Oh, she thought, it is a lovely one! I'm not going to throw that one away. She slipped it into her dress pocket to take home. She would put it with the other treasures gathered in her walks with Uncle Asa.

Laura began to feel around for a stone that was not so nice to throw in the brook. This time she found a rough piece of granite and threw it in the direction in which she knew the water lay. Then she wondered whether it really had hit the water. She found a large rock and let it drop directly below her. Laura smiled as the cold water splashed up on her legs. She knew that one had surely hit the water!

Now Uncle Asa pulled on Laura's arm. She knew that meant that it was time to start for home. She had already noticed that the sun did not feel as warm as it had earlier in the afternoon. Probably it was nearing suppertime. Uncle Asa helped her up off the warm rock on which they had been sitting.

As they followed the narrow path that the cows had made from the brook over to the wagon road, Uncle Asa led the way. He held back the long blackberry brambles and guided Laura carefully. He had to guide Laura because she was blind. She had been blind ever since she was two years old. At that time she had nearly died of scarlet fever.

Laura and Uncle Asa did not say anything as they walked along. If Uncle Asa had said anything, Laura could not have heard him because she was completely deaf. The fever had made her deaf as well as blind.

And Laura did not say anything to Uncle Asa either, because she could not talk. A person who cannot talk is called mute. At the time when Laura lived children who became deaf before they had learned to talk always became mute. They never learned to speak.

This little girl who could not see or hear or talk was named Laura Bridgman. She was a real little girl and she lived almost 150 years ago in Mill Village, a part of Hanover, New Hampshire. She was born on December 21, 1829. Although as a tiny baby she was not very strong, still she had been able to see and hear. By the time she was two years old she was beginning to say a few words, just as most children do.

And then the dreadful sickness had come. For several months after the fever Laura had lain in a large old cradle in a darkened room. Gradually her father and mother discovered that the sickness had made her blind and deaf. For weeks she could only drink liquids and could not even sit up. It was a whole year before she could walk by herself again and it was not until she was about five years old that she was nearly as strong as most children her age.

Perhaps she would never have become very healthy if it had not been for her friend Mr. Asa Tenney. The Bridgman family called him Uncle Asa, but he was not a real uncle to them. Most people thought that Asa Tenney was a little queer. Although he seemed very old, he wasn't, really. But his clothes were. He didn't care about things like clothes. All he cared about were out-of-door things — like birds and flowers and brooks, and the little dumb animals that he found on his walks.

And now he had come to care about Laura Bridgman, too. In a way she seemed almost like one of the little helpless creatures of the woods. Like them, she could not tell people what she was thinking and what she wanted. But he knew that she wanted kindness and attention and love.

Mr. Tenney had no family of his own. When he discovered this little girl at neighbor Bridgman's house he felt that at last he had found someone who needed him.

Daniel and Harmony Bridgman, Laura's father and mother, were kindly people and wanted to do what they could for this poor child of theirs. But they had little time to give her. Mr. Bridgman was a busy farmer and a selectman of the town of Hanover. Mrs. Bridgman had two little boys younger than Laura to care for. In addition, she had to do all the things that any farm wife did in those days.

She had a flock of sheep that must be tended. Their wool had to be spun and made into cloth. She also spun and wove flax. This cloth and the woolen cloth had to be made into clothes for her family. Mrs. Bridgman also kept bees and

chickens. She made soap and candles and all of her own bread. And, of course, there were all the meals to get and all the washing and ironing to do.

In most farm homes a large family was a fine thing to have because the children could begin to help at an early age. But Laura's two older sisters had died from scarlet fever at the time Laura was sick. Now there were no older children to help this busy mother.

No, Mrs. Bridgman did not have much time to teach her little deaf, blind, mute daughter. Even if there had been time, how could she have taught Laura anything? Can a person who cannot see or hear or talk learn anything?

Asa Tenney was sure Laura could learn. He believed that she was learning every minute and that she wanted to learn a great deal more. He knew that he had plenty of time in which to teach her, too.

He explained it to himself this way: "It is as though Laura is living in a room without windows or doors. I must make windows and doors into that room. Somehow, I must get behind the cloth band that she wears over her eyes and bring the light of understanding to her."

JUST AS SOON as Laura was well enough to be out of doors much, Uncle Asa had begun taking her on excursions. At first they were short ones, just around the farm itself. On these first walks he carried Laura a good part of the time. But as she grew stronger the two friends were able to go farther and farther in their explorations.

Uncle Asa knew that he could not tell Laura what they were seeing or where they were going, and so he let the world itself do the telling. That is why, when they visited the brook in winter, he let Laura walk on the ice and feel it hard and cold under her feet. And that is why, when they were at the brook this day, he found a long stick and let her feel the wildly rushing water pull it.

Now, as they walked toward the Bridgman farm late on this lovely May day, Uncle Asa saw another way in which the world itself could tell Laura that spring had come to New Hampshire.

A big mother robin was sitting high on an apple tree in the orchard at the side of the road. She was shouting out her "Cheerio, cheer-up, cheerily," just as loudly as possible. A fat father robin was standing in the road ahead. He was tugging a plump worm out of a wet wagon rut. There, now he had him, and father robin flew straight to the tree where mother robin was singing. He disappeared below her among the blossom-covered branches.

Of course Laura could not see or hear any of these things. But Uncle Asa had carefully noticed just exactly where the father bird disappeared among the branches. He touched Laura's arm. She understood what he meant by that touch. She was to stand perfectly still and wait right where she was at the side of the road until he came back.

He started over into the orchard. Quickly he climbed into the low crotch of the tree on which the mother robin was singing. The singing stopped. Uncle Asa went on climbing until he came to the branch where he thought the father robin had gone in. As he brushed back the branches, there was a quick flutter of wings and the father robin flew out. Then as Uncle Asa leaned on the branch he was greeted with a loud chorus of peeps.

"Ho, ho! Just as I thought — a family of baby robins. Yes, there's the nest, and, let me see — one, two, three, four babies."

The baby birds seemed to be about two weeks old. They were not all naked as newly hatched birds are, but had plenty of feathers. Their eyes were open and so were their mouths!

"Peep, peep, peep, peep," they shouted, their long skinny necks stretched tall and their mouths wide open. They thought Uncle Asa was their mother or father bringing them worms. Each one wanted to be sure to get a good big mouthful!

"Sorry, little birds," said Uncle Asa, "I don't have anything for you. I just wanted to know exactly where you were. I want my little friend Laura to meet one of you. We won't hurt you. I'm sure if you could understand all about Laura you wouldn't mind a bit. I'll be back in a minute."

Uncle Asa climbed down the tree and walked over to the wagon road where Laura stood waiting. He took her hand and led her into the orchard. He helped her find a comfortable place to sit, in the grass by the trunk of the tree.

The mother and father robin were both quite

upset by the return of this visitor to their nurs-
ery. They were far up in the branches of the
tree making the worried cry that robins make at
such times. They kept up their troubled calling
as Uncle Asa climbed up again to the branch
which held their nest.

Very carefully and gently he lifted out one
baby robin. "Peep, peep, peep," it cried. Never
before had it felt a person's hand and it didn't
think it liked it one bit.

"Don't you worry, little bird, I'll put you
back in just a few minutes," and Uncle Asa
climbed down the tree with the frightened bird
cuddled close to him.

With his free hand he arranged Laura's hands
in the shape of a cup. Then he put the live ball of
feathers in the nest made of hands.

A smile spread across Laura's face. She had
learned to expect surprises like this on her walks
with Uncle Asa. She felt the warm bird, so soft

and frightened. Of course she could not hear the peeping noises it was making, but she could feel the quick beating of its heart and the wild flapping of its tiny wings.

Little by little Laura had learned that with small, soft, breathing things she must be very,

very careful. Once, when she was younger, Uncle Asa had brought a tiny animal to her to hold. It was a baby rabbit. She had been so excited that she had grabbed it tightly around the neck and, before Uncle Asa could rescue it, she had stopped its breathing. Now Laura knew that if she were gentle with such things, they would go on breathing and feeling warm.

Sometimes Uncle Asa caught funny slippery creatures down by the brook. They were not warm, but they wiggled and kicked. Laura had learned to hold frogs tightly enough so that they could not jump out of her hands and yet not so tightly that they could never jump out again.

Of course Laura did not know the names we use for any of these things — birds or rabbits or frogs. She just knew the things themselves.

The little bird in Laura's hands did not seem so frightened now. It was crouched down and breathing heavily, but it was no longer flapping its wings. Laura could feel the bird's claws curled around her fingers. She felt the little beak peck at her hands, but she was not afraid. She even put her cheek close to the soft back for a moment to feel the downy feathers on her skin. Laura could feel softness just as well as you or I can.

Uncle Asa could hear the mother and father robin still uttering their worried cries in the tree above. He decided that it was time to return the baby bird to its nest. Taking the bird from Laura, he climbed up the tree once more and put it back with the others.

"Thank you, little bird. I'm sure Laura loved holding you even though you may not have loved being held. Laura and I will go right home now and your mother and father can come and feed you."

Back to the wagon road walked the two friends and up the hill toward the Bridgman farm. The sun was really low now and the sky

was layered with pink and red and gray. Laura could not see how beautiful it was and there was no way that Uncle Asa could show that beauty to her.

Now he could see the smoke rising from the Bridgman chimney. Another turn of the road brought them within sight of the house itself.

Uncle Asa stopped short. That stranger's horse was tied outside the Bridgman farm again!

Laura could tell that something was troubling her good friend. She waited patiently until he was ready to start on. She could not hear him muttering crossly to himself: "I don't like him. Why is he always watching Laura? I wish he'd go away and stay away!"

When they arrived at the door of the house, Uncle Asa knocked heavily before opening the door and going in.

"I thought that must be you and Laura," said Mrs. Bridgman, looking up. "You must be tired and hungry, Asa. Won't you stay and have supper with us tonight? Mr. Barrett will be with us again and one more guest is no trouble."

"No, thank you, Mrs. Bridgman," said Uncle Asa, "I must be getting right home. I have my chores to do and I'll want to turn in early."

As he started to go a young man came across the room. "Good evening, Mr. Tenney. I do wish you would accept Mrs. Bridgman's invitation. You could tell us all about what you and Laura have been doing. Her cheeks are so rosy that I'm sure she has had a wonderful time."

"No, I must go," said Uncle Asa, rather gruffly.

"Well, I'm sure that if Laura could thank you she would," said the young man. "She is a lucky little girl to have such a wonderful friend."

"Hmph!" said Uncle Asa. "Who wants thanks? I don't. Laura's company is the only thanks I want. But I do want that!" And he hurried out the door toward home.

As soon as Laura came into the big farm kitchen she found her little rocking chair and settled herself in it. The chair was in its usual place, drawn up at one side of the huge fireplace.

The air had grown chill toward the end of the afternoon and now the fire felt good to Laura. This fire had to be kept going almost all the time, even in warm weather. It was not only the family furnace but also the family cookstove. Mrs.

Bridgman did all of her cooking either in the hot coals or on kettles hung from the crane or in the big oven in the back of the fireplace.

She was busy cooking supper now, stirring something in one large kettle, looking quickly into another. As Laura sat rocking she could not smell the good smells that filled the kitchen. Her sense of smell had also been almost completely destroyed by the fever that made her deaf and blind. But she could feel the warmth of the fire and she could feel the comfortable rhythm of her own rocking.

In another minute she could feel something else, too. Patches, the family cat, hopped up into her lap. There was no place that Patches liked better for her long snoozes than Laura's lap. And Laura loved to have the big family pet take her naps there. She could not see the different-colored patches of fur that gave the cat her name, but she could feel the deep softness of the fur. And although Laura could not hear the steady purring of the contented cat, she could feel it through the fur.

Thanks to her walks with Uncle Asa, Laura knew more about living things now. She knew that cats like to sit beside the fire but not *in* the fire. Once, when she was much younger, she had thrown the family cat, Blackie, right into the fire. The poor creature had been badly burned

before Mrs. Bridgman was able to rescue it, and then it had run away and never come back. Laura would never again do such a thing to something alive. She knew better now. She was glad to have her friend Patches use her lap as a bed.

But now another friend was looking for a bed. Laura's youngest brother, Addison, came toddling across the room. "Laura home," he told his mother as he clambered up into Laura's lap. Patches moved over. She was used to sharing her comfortable bed with Addison.

In just a few minutes the warm fire, the regular rocking, and the steady purring of the cat put little brother to sleep. Laura could tell he was asleep even though she could not see his drowsy eyes close. She felt his head drop heavily on her arm and his fat little hand that rested in hers lie still.

In a moment more Laura might have dropped off to sleep too. But just then her mother came

over and took sleepy little brother from her lap.
Mrs. Bridgman put him in the large cradle that
stood in a corner of the room. This was the
cradle in which Laura had slept as a baby and in
which she had lain sick for so many months.

Then Mrs. Bridgman brushed the cat from Laura's lap and placed some spoons in her daughter's hand. Laura knew that her mother was asking her to set the table for supper. She was glad to help when she could and setting the table was one thing that she could do easily and well.

She knew that her father's place was at the head of the table. Next to him on one side she very often set an extra place for Uncle Asa or some other guest. If there was to be a guest her mother gave her the necessary number of extra spoons. Tonight Mr. Barrett would sit in the guest's seat. On the other side of her father Laura set her own place. Laura sat near her father so that he could give her help as she needed it during a meal.

Then Laura set her mother's place at the other end of the table. On either side of her mother she set places for her two little brothers. Laura knew exactly where to find the forks and knives that were needed. She could also find the nap-

kins and plates by herself. She knew that one very dented pewter plate belonged to her four-year-old brother, John, and the other plate that was slightly less dented to her two-year-old brother, Addison.

And of course she knew her own plate. It had been a present from Uncle Asa. There were decorations around the outer edge of the plate — the letters of the alphabet raised up so that Laura could feel them. Often, as she sat silently at the table during a long meal, she traced their outlines with her fingertip. She wondered what the lines were. Would she ever know?

While Laura was setting the table James Barrett, the young man who was there, watched her. He had come to think that Laura was the most amazing little girl he had ever seen. The more he had a chance to watch her, the more wonderful he thought she was.

James Barrett was a student at Dartmouth College in Hanover. He was doing part-time work for Mr. Bridgman in order to earn some extra money. A selectman like Mr. Bridgman helps to run the business of a small town. James Barrett had been hired to help with some of the many records that a selectman must keep.

He had noticed Laura on the very first day that he had come from Hanover to work. At first, although he could see that she was not just like other children, he did not know all of the reasons. Gradually he discovered that she was blind, deaf and mute. When he felt that he knew Mrs. Bridgman well enough, he asked her about Laura and she told him the whole sad story.

Day after day as he sat working on the town records at a table in the kitchen, he could not help but stop at frequent intervals to watch Laura. The thing that made her seem so remarkable was that she did not just sit in a chair all day, as he rather expected such a child would, but instead moved about the house and farm eager to learn and to know what was going on.

Although she could not hear or see her mother as she busily did her many chores, Laura could feel the floor or even the air vibrate as her mother moved about. Catching hold of her mother's skirts she would follow her. If Mrs. Bridgman were making bread and kneading the dough, Laura would place her hands on her mother's arms and knead it with her. Sometimes her mother gave her a lump of dough to knead and shape by herself. Often Laura worked along with her mother as she spun, wove cloth on her heavy loom, or did the churning.

As James Barrett watched Laura he wondered about many things. Perhaps someday he would be a teacher. How would he set about teaching such a child? We learn, he reflected to himself, by thinking, by using our brains. But what makes our brains work? Our eyes send picture messages to our brains and so we think about what we are seeing. But Laura's eyes don't send any messages to her brain.

Our ears send sound messages to our brains, he thought. But Laura's ears don't send any messages to her brain. Our noses and the taste buds on our tongues send messages about smells and tastes to our brains, but Mrs. Bridgman has

old me that Laura can smell and taste almost
nothing. She will take the most horrid-tasting
and -smelling medicine without showing any
signs of having tasted or smelled it.

So what keeps a person like Laura thinking
and exploring? pondered young James Barrett.
How is the world getting into her mind? Only
through her sense of touch. Whatever she can
feel with her hands, her feet, or the skin all over
her body can get to her brain.

Laura certainly used her hands. They were
almost never still. How could she let them rest

when they had to do the work of her four useless senses as well as their own work? They had no time to waste. They were constantly reaching out, feeling everything they lighted upon, and feeling for things they had not yet found.

Soon after James Barrett had come to help Mr. Bridgman Laura had discovered him working at the table by the kitchen window. Immediately she had begun feeling his clothes, his hands, and up toward his face.

Then Laura's father had stamped his foot. Instantly Laura had stopped her explorations. She had learned that when her father stamped like that it meant she must stop whatever she was doing. If she didn't, her father became very cross. James Barrett wondered how Laura had "heard" her father stamp his foot. Mr. Bridgman explained that she had felt the floor vibrate. She was "hearing" with her feet.

Later that day, when Mr. Bridgman had gone out, James Barrett had let Laura feel his face.

'After all," he explained to Mrs. Bridgman, "that is the only way in which Laura can know what I look like. She has to 'see' me through her fingers. Even a child who can really see, if he is allowed, wants to touch things at first so he can know more about them. How much more important it is for little Laura to be able to feel things!"

James Barrett had decided that one reason Laura learned so much in her walks with Asa Tenney was because he let her feel and handle and touch so many different things. He wished that Mr. Tenney would be more friendly toward him. He wanted to talk with him about Laura. He wanted to ask him many questions about his ways of teaching her.

But no! The minute he started to ask him anything about Laura, Mr. Tenney would become cold and unfriendly and start for home. Anyone could see that he loved Laura. Then why didn't he want to talk about her?

Now, as Laura was setting the table, James Barrett spoke to Mrs. Bridgman about this. "It was the same way again tonight, did you notice? The minute I began to show some interest in Laura he got almost angry with me. Why? Why should he?"

"I think I know," said Mrs. Bridgman slowly. "Poor Asa has had a lonely life with no family of his own for years. Until he found Laura he had no one to love and to take care of except the baby birds he found fallen from their nests, or a hurt rabbit, or some other helpless creature. In Laura he has found someone who really needs him. I think he is afraid that somehow he'll lose Laura if you become interested in her."

"Poor old man," said James Barrett. "I don't know why he thinks he might lose Laura because of me. I don't know where he thinks I could take her. There aren't any schools for children like Laura. At least, I don't think there are."

LAURA HAD finished setting the table for her mother, but Mr. Bridgman had not yet come in from the evening chores. Laura went over to one corner of the kitchen where there was an old cabinet.

James Barrett was watching her and he knew why she went there. That was where she kept her very strange "doll." It was not a real doll, but an old leather boot that she often held in her lap. She seemed to think of it as a doll. She rocked it and cuddled it in much the same way that she held her little brother.

It was this boot that Laura had gone to get. James Barrett watched her. First she found a large key on a shelf near the cabinet. With the key she opened a low door in the cabinet. She had learned that she must keep this door locked if her boot were to be safe from her two little brothers.

Taking her boot she went over and sat down in her rocking chair. She reached into her skirt pocket and took out the smooth stone that she had found on her afternoon walk. He watched her feel it and brush it against her cheek. Then he saw her take her boot and turn it gently on its side.

Out onto her lap rolled several small objects. James Barrett already knew what they were— treasures found on her walks with Uncle Asa. There were several stones. One was flat and shiny. He watched Laura peel off a thin layer of the stone. No matter how many times she peeled off a layer there always seemed to be another one. This was mica. He wished that Laura could see as well as feel this amazing "stone."

The next one of her treasures was a blue-jay feather. She drew it through her fingers, making all the barbs go in one direction. After a few minutes she laid it down and picked up something that looked like a toothpick. It was round and smooth, white at one end and black at the other. He had asked Mrs. Bridgman what it was one day and she had said it was a porcupine quill. Laura had let him feel it. It was as soft and smooth as silk, until he touched the tip of it.

That had a tiny hook on the end. Laura was careful to avoid touching that.

The next treasure that Laura took out was a fat, bumpy, dull green thing. Some white fluff was coming out of it. This was a milkweed pod. Laura and Uncle Asa had found it in the fall. Now it was dry and brittle on the outside. Laura ran her fingers over the silky down attached to the seeds. How soft it was! Some of the seeds had escaped and lay loose among the treasures on her lap. She carefully tucked them back into the pod. In the fall, when she and Uncle Asa were walking in the fields they had found lots of these pods. Sometimes he made her blow at them. Laura wondered why.

Now James Barrett watched as Laura took out a small object and ran her finger around and around on it. That must be the empty snail shell they had found last week. He had watched Laura and Uncle Asa as they sat on the granite doorstep by the kitchen. Uncle Asa had held

Laura's hand and helped her trace the spiral shape of the shell with one finger. James Barrett wondered what her brain could think as her fingers traced the spiral pattern. What is a spiral to a mind that has never seen one?

Finally Laura reached into the toe of the boot and brought out a tiny box. She took out a large section of a broken robin's egg. Some mother robin had thrown it out of the nest after a baby robin had pecked its way out. Mother robins are good housekeepers! Laura could not see the lovely blue coloring of the shell but she could feel its smoothness.

Suddenly Laura stopped feeling her treasures and looked up. She was listening and hearing something, not with her ears, but with her whole body. She knew that the door of the farm kitchen had opened and then closed. Probably it was her father coming in. Laura went back to her treasures.

But so did someone else! Brother John had

come up beside Laura and had taken one of her treasures. Too late, Laura felt his hand in her lap. Quick as lightning she reached out for his hand, but he was even quicker. Laura felt wildly about in the air. There! She had him by the arm. She gripped him as tightly as she could.

Brother John began to bellow. Of course, Laura could not hear him. Frightened, he dropped the shell and in a moment more had stepped on it. Laura was shaking him with the hand that gripped him and feeling about for her treasures with the other hand. John went on screaming.

Suddenly Laura stopped shaking him, although she did not loosen her hold. She had felt her father stamp his foot. There, he stamped it again. She knew that she should let go of her brother. But he had taken one of her treasures. She was sure he had. No! She would not let go of him, not until he gave it back. They were hers! She hung on to him. She began shaking him again.

A moment later Laura felt her father's powerful hand take hold of her. She felt a blow on her hand that was clutching her brother and she let go. But now she was like a furious wild animal. All of her treasures were being scattered on the floor. She began crying and making the strange, unpleasant sound that she could and did make when upset. Again she felt a blow from her father's powerful hand and she fell in a limp ball on the floor, sobbing.

Laura could not hear her father apologizing to James Barrett for the dreadful behavior of his daughter. "I don't know what we can do," said Mr. Bridgman. "She always used to obey me the moment I stamped my foot, but now she has become more willful. I do not like to strike her, but scenes such as this have occurred more and more of late."

James Barrett was listening respectfully to Mr. Bridgman's apology. But he was also looking for Laura's scattered treasures. Fearful that Mr. Bridgman might take offense, nonetheless he tried to defend Laura.

"I saw it all happen, sir. She was playing with her treasures when John crept up and snatched one from her lap. Had I been quicker I might have stopped him. Don't be too harsh with the child. She is a truly wonderful little girl."

In silence Mr. Bridgman turned away to prepare himself for supper. James Barrett searched the floor and found the stones, the milkweed pod, the feather, and in between the wide boards of the floor the porcupine quill. Alas, the robin's egg shell and the snail shell lay crushed. He found Laura's boot and helped her place the stones, seed pod, feather and quill back inside, but he could not make her understand what had happened to the shells.

The boot was placed back on the shelf and the

cupboard locked with the big key. The family and guest gathered around the supper table.

"I fear," said Mr. Bridgman, "that Laura will become more and more like a wild animal. She was the smartest of any of our children before this dreadful affliction came upon her. Now, I am afraid, she cannot be taught anything."

As HE RODE his horse back to college that evening, James Barrett could think of nothing but Laura Bridgman. He did not hear the robins singing their late "cheerio-cheer-up's." He did not see the apple blossoms that covered the orchard trees so that there seemed to be great vases of flowers along the road. He did not smell the blossom-laden lilac bushes that stood by the farmhouse doors as he rode past. For the time being it was almost as if he too were deaf and blind and dull of senses, his thoughts were so busy with Laura Bridgman.

Of course she is becoming more and more disobedient! thought James Barrett to himself. She is so bright and so interested in things that she cannot be easily held back. She knew that those were her very own treasures and that little John would spoil them. She disobeyed her father because she cared so much about them. If only she could tell people what she wants and why she does things. But she can't! She probably never can!

Even a night's sleep did not entirely clear James Barrett's mind of such thoughts. He went to his first class at college in the morning only half prepared in his lessons and not able to concentrate on what the teacher was saying. The class was one in anatomy, the study of the human body, and the teacher was Dr. Reuben Mussey. Dr. Mussey was one of James Barrett's favorite teachers and it suddenly occurred to James that Dr. Mussey might be interested in hearing about Laura.

After the class was over he told Dr. Mussey all about Laura Bridgman. He was glad to be able to share his enthusiasm and concern for this remarkable little girl with someone outside the family.

"I just wish that you would come out to the Bridgman farm with me sometime, sir, and see her for yourself. It is just amazing to me that she knows as much as she does."

"Well, James," said Dr. Mussey, "I would indeed be very much interested in seeing this child. You know how much I feel we have still to discover about the human body and mind, and how they work. But do you think that the Bridgmans would welcome my coming? They might think I was just curious."

"I believe that Mr. Bridgman would be most happy to have you come, especially if he thought that you might be able to help in some way. After all, he knows how difficult it is to make Laura obey him now. He knows he needs help."

"I wish that I thought I really could be of some assistance," said Dr. Mussey, "but I doubt that there is anything much that can be done for such a child. Your enthusiasm makes me want to see her, however, if you are sure that no one will mind my coming."

"Well," said James Barrett, "I can't truthfully say that *no one* will mind. Mr. and Mrs. Bridgman won't, I'm sure, but Mr. Tenney will probably mind a good deal." And James Barrett told Dr. Mussey all about Laura's wonderful but suspicious friend.

Professor Mussey was very much interested in what James Barrett told him about Mr. Tenney. "He must be a remarkable teacher. I would like to see him and Laura together. He has probably found many ways to communicate with her other than through words. See if you can arrange a visit to the Bridgmans' at a time when Mr. Tenney will be there also."

The next week, on Thursday, Dr. Mussey and James Barrett drove together to the Bridgman farm. They arrived in the early afternoon, having been invited to remain for supper also.

Mrs. Bridgman told them that Laura and Uncle Asa were out in the back meadow feeding the sheep. They walked around behind the big barn and looked across to the meadow. A flock of sheep was grazing there.

"I don't want Mr. Tenney to think that we are spying on him," said James Barrett, "but I'm afraid that if he sees us right away he'll just bring Laura back to the house and go home. There they are, do you see them?"

"Yes, I see them," said Dr. Mussey. "Let's start over in their direction. Both of them have their backs to us and seem very busy with something. Perhaps they won't notice us for a bit."

As they came closer they could see that Uncle Asa had brought a pewter bottle of milk. He was taking it out of his jacket pocket. They watched as he gave it to Laura. She sat right down in the grass with it and a young, still wobbly-legged little lamb came running over to her.

The lamb went down on its knees in front of her. Laura popped the bottle of milk into its mouth.

"Even a child who can see and hear couldn't have more fun than that," said Dr. Mussey. "They must have done this many times before. Laura knew just what to do. Let's go over there, James. I want to meet Mr. Tenney. Surely he won't go off and leave Laura feeding the lamb alone."

James Barrett was not at all sure that Asa Ten-

ney would not leave when *he* came into sight,
but he took Dr. Mussey over anyway. Laura,
busy with the lamb, did not notice their arrival
in any way.

"Mr. Tenney," said James Barrett, "I would
like to introduce Dr. Mussey. He is one of my
teachers at the college. I have told him a great
deal about you and Laura."

Uncle Asa did not look at all pleased at the
arrival of a second stranger who was interested in
Laura. It was bad enough having James Barrett
watching Laura so much, and now he was bringing his friends to see her too!

"How do you do," he said quite gruffly.
"Laura's busy feeding an orphan lamb, as you
can see."

Dr. Mussey shook hands with Mr. Tenney
and then he asked, "Why doesn't one of the
other mother sheep feed this baby?"

"Sheep are funny that way," said Uncle Asa,
forgetting to be unfriendly for a minute. "They

don't like to adopt another ewe's baby, even if it is motherless."

"I didn't realize that," said Dr. Mussey. "What kind of sheep are these?"

Uncle Asa's face began to brighten. This stranger seemed much more interested in farm animals than in Laura. After Laura had finished feeding the lamb, they went to the barn to gather eggs. Dr. Mussey wanted to know just what kind of hens they were and how many eggs they usually laid each day. When they visited the pigs he wanted to know what the pigs had been fed to make them so fat so early in the year.

In a very short time Dr. Mussey and Asa Tenney were the best of friends. James Barrett went back to the farmhouse to do some of his regular work on Mr. Bridgman's papers. Uncle Asa and Laura and Dr. Mussey finished the chores, explored the woods at the edge of the meadow and just generally had a fine time.

Dr. Mussey didn't ask a single question about

Laura. But that didn't mean that he wasn't interested in her or that he wasn't finding out a great deal. But he knew something that young James Barrett did not know. He knew that if he seemed to show no interest in Laura, Mr. Tenney would not feel frightened and uneasy. At the same time, because Laura was right there with them, Uncle Asa couldn't help but show Dr. Mussey some of his ways of teaching her.

Dr. Mussey was also able to see that Laura and Uncle Asa had a kind of sign language that they used with each other. For example, a slight push meant that they were going somewhere, a pull meant that she wanted to show him something. If she raised her hand to her lips it meant that she wanted a drink from the well. If she sat down as they were walking it meant that she was tired and wanted to rest. There were many other signs that passed between Uncle Asa and Laura that a person less interested than Dr. Mussey might not have noticed.

One thing was very clear to him: Laura was indeed a very bright little girl and she could use her mind wonderfully well in spite of being deaf, blind, mute and almost without a sense of taste or smell. Before they sat down to supper Dr. Mussey was able to carry out a few simple tests on Laura about which he wrote a report sometime later. At the end of this report he said: "She was considered by her parents as unusually intelligent before her sickness, and is still so regarded by them."

In a short time Mrs. Bridgman called her family and the three guests to supper. Mr. Tenney, Dr. Mussey and Mr. Bridgman were soon busily engaged in conversation. James Barrett had been careful to take a place next to Laura. As the others were talking, James took Laura's little hand and guided it over to something beside his plate.

Laura's face brightened. James Barrett was helping her trace the spiral shape on a new snail shell; one of her lost treasures had mysteriously returned! Then he placed something close to her other hand: the smooth, rounded end of a large section of a robin's egg! Again a smile spread over Laura's face; her second lost treasure was found.

Little did Laura know how many hours James Barrett had spent when he should have been studying, looking under damp rocks for an empty snail shell and under apple trees for a section of an eggshell, thrown from the nest by some busy mother robin. When the meal was over he helped Laura put her treasures safely away in her boot.

As Dr. Mussey and James Barrett rode back through the lush green New Hampshire countryside, Dr. Mussey said, "I have a plan, James; let's see what comes of it."

YOUNG DR. Samuel Gridley Howe was sitting
reading by a window in his apartment. For five
years he had been the director of the first school
for the blind in the United States. This school
in Boston, Massachusetts, was called the New
England Asylum for the Blind. It had been
founded in 1829 by Dr. John D. Fisher. In 1832
Dr. Howe had been appointed the first director.

In five years he had seen the school grow from
a few rooms in his own father's home with just
a handful of pupils to a real school housed in a
beautiful mansion, a gift from wealthy Colonel
Thomas Perkins. Later, when the school was
moved to even larger quarters in South Boston,

it was renamed Perkins Institution. Moved again, in 1912, to Watertown, Massachusetts, it is now known all over the world as Perkins School for the Blind.

At this time Dr. Howe was not married and lived with his unmarried sister, Miss Jeannette Howe, in a small apartment in the school. Miss Jeannette, as everyone called her, was busy sewing as Dr. Howe sat reading by the window. The cool June breeze felt refreshing to the tired young director who took his job so seriously.

Suddenly he became very excited about something he was reading. "By Jove!" he said, aloud. "She sounds like just the child I have been hoping to find."

"Who does?" asked Miss Jeannete, looking up from her sewing. "What child have you been hoping to find?"

"There is a report here," said the young doctor, "written by my friend Dr. Reuben Mussey of Dartmouth College. It tells of a remarkable child who has recently been brought to his attention. She lives on a farm in the outskirts of Hanover. The child has been deaf, blind, mute and practically without a sense of taste or smell since the age of two. He reports quite fully about his visit to observe her in her home and says that in spite of these many handicaps she is an unusually alert and clever child."

"What is her name?" asked Miss Jeannette.

"Her name is Laura Bridgman. She is seven years old and in good health. She does simple household tasks as well as chores about the farm. She even sews and knits with some skill. But most important of all, he says she is as eager to learn and as curious about all that goes on around her as any normal seven-year-old. He wonders if perhaps she could not be educated.

"Jeannette, you know how eager I have been to find a child like this and to experiment with some of my ideas about the education of the deaf-blind. I am sure that she is the one I should begin with."

"But Sam," said Miss Jeannette, "don't you have enough to do now without attempting such a hopeless task? You know how unsuccessful they have been in the attempt to educate Julia Brace down in Hartford. She too is deaf, blind and mute. She just doesn't seem to want to learn."

"That is just the point," said Dr. Howe. "This child *is* eager to learn, according to Dr. Mussey's report. Her own curiosity and eagerness will be as important as anything I will be able to do. Don't forget, Julia Brace was nearly thirty years old when they attempted to educate her. Seven is a golden age for learning. I am determined to go to Hanover and see this child myself. If Dr. Mussey is right about her ability, and I know what a careful observer he is, I intend to seek her parents' permission to bring her here to the school in the fall."

"Well, I only hope that you are not going to be disappointed, Sam," said Miss Jeannette.

"I feel sure that I won't be," said Dr. Howe enthusiastically. "I'll write Dr. Mussey tonight and ask him to make arrangements for me to visit the little girl in July. Our school will be having vacation. I had thought of going to the graduation at Dartmouth then, anyhow."

It was an excited Dr. Mussey who, a few days later, reported to an equally excited James Barrett the arrival of a letter from the distinguished Dr. Samuel Gridley Howe.

"He says," Dr. Mussey explained, "that there has never been a child as handicapped as Laura educated at his school. He says that, to his knowledge, no deaf, blind and mute person has ever been successfully educated anywhere.

But he has been eager to try to educate just such a child. I think our Laura is going to have her chance."

The very next day Dr. Mussey made a visit to the Bridgman farm and received permission to bring Dr. Howe to see Laura in July. He explained that Dr. Howe was hopeful about the possibility of educating her at his school.

Mr. and Mrs. Bridgman were most grateful to Dr. Mussey. They were realizing more acutely each day that unless something were done soon for their intelligent little daughter she would become wholly unmanageable.

But Dr. Mussey was not able to convince Asa Tenney that any good would come from Dr. Howe's visit. Uncle Asa was certain that he himself could teach Laura all that she would ever need to know.

"Haven't I taught her to love the creatures of the woods and the flowers of the fields?" he asked Dr. Mussey. "She has waded in the brook

in summer, slid on the ice in winter and felt its power when it is swollen in the spring. She has raised lambs, learned to find the hidden nests of hens and held newborn kittens and puppies in her hands.

"I have taught her in the only way that she can learn — through her hands. What can they teach her in a school? Teachers whom she cannot hear using books that she cannot see! The great out-of-doors is the best schoolroom there is for any child, but even more so for Laura."

"Yes, Asa," said Dr. Mussey, "what you have done for Laura is wonderful. Without your teaching no other teacher would be able to do anything. You have kept alive her curiosity and eagerness to learn. You have given her wonderful experiences. But you yourself have seen what is happening more and more often now. She flies into a rage and is almost like a caged animal when she wants something but cannot make those around her understand *what* she wants."

Asa Tenney looked uncomfortably down at the ground. He knew exactly what Dr. Mussey meant. Just a few days before, he and Laura had gone out to salt the sheep. Laura had wanted to feed the baby lamb a bottle of milk again. Uncle Asa had no way of telling her that the lamb had now grown too big and could feed itself. Determined little Laura had searched in every one of Uncle Asa's pockets for the bottle of milk and, furious at not finding it, had reached up and caught hold of his glasses. She had torn them off his face and crushed them on the ground.

"You do not want Mr. Bridgman to have to treat her like a dumb animal, whipping her if she will not obey him," said Dr. Mussey gently. "Dr. Howe believes that Laura can be taught to understand our words and to talk with us. Surely you, who have set her free this far, won't stand in the way of giving her even greater freedom?"

"Oh, I have nothing to say about it," said Asa Tenney in despair. "If Mr. Bridgman thinks that this Dr. Howe can make a blind child see, a deaf child hear and a mute child talk, who am I to contradict him?"

"He too will have to work through Laura's hands, Asa, just as you have," said Dr. Mussey. "Those wonderful hands that you have helped to make so sensitive."

But nothing that was said could convince Asa Tenney that sending Laura to school in Boston was going to be a good thing. And nothing would induce him to be on hand on the afternoon when the carriage with Dr. Mussey and Dr. Howe arrived at the Bridgman farm.

Laura never forgot her first meeting with Dr. Samuel Gridley Howe. He was an unusually tall man and she was just a little girl. His great height combined with his great gentleness made a lasting impression. When he took her small hand in his large one on that July afternoon in New Hampshire there began an adventure in education that was to become famous all over the United States and parts of Europe.

Even in the short visit that he made that day Dr. Howe caught a glimpse of Laura Bridgman's unusual quickness and intelligence. Like James Barrett and Dr. Mussey before him he was much impressed, and knew that Laura Bridgman was the child with whom to carry on his first experiment in the education of the deaf-blind.

As a result of the visit it was agreed that Laura would go to Dr. Howe's school in the fall.

It was Columbus Day, October 12, 1837, just a few weeks before her eighth birthday, when Laura Bridgman started out on her great adventure. Seated in a light carriage, called a chaise, between her father and mother, Laura was tense with excitement. Where was she going? No one could tell her.

Why had she helped her mother put the best of her old clothes and many new ones in a large trunk that she knew was in the carriage with them? Why had her treasures been taken out of her boot and put in a box in among her clothes?

Laura knew that something very unusual was happening. Exactly what it was she did not know, but at least her parents were with her.

Of course she could not see how beautiful Hanover was on this October day. As yet there had been no killing frost and the late autumn flowers, especially the goldenrod and asters, were lovely. The sugar maples were at the peak of their golden glory and the red maples were brilliant to the seeing eye. The woodbine curled like tongues of fire up and around the trees along the road. Laura did not know that she was saying goodbye to all this beauty for a while.

But there was someone who did know. From a rise of ground in the back meadow Asa Tenney watched the chaise drive away from the Bridgman farm. There were tears in his eyes. How right he had been to think that no good could come from the visits of that first stranger, James Barrett. No good had come! Laura was being taken away from him. His worst fears had come true.

This October there would be no one to take tramping through the piles of fallen maple leaves.

There would be no one for whom to gather fat milkweed pods. And why should he bother this year to find the plumpest apples in the orchard or the fallen hickory nuts along the stone wall?

Laura was gone. The light had gone out of Asa Tenney's life. It was never to be lighted quite so brightly again. Although Laura did visit home and Uncle Asa saw her many times, it was never the same again for him.

But a light was soon to be lighted in the life of Laura Bridgman that was to shine into the lives of deaf-blind children all over the world. And because of the hours he had spent taking a little deaf-blind child to the meadows and woods, the name of Asa Tenney has not been forgotten.

The trip from Hanover to Boston was a long one in those days. The Bridgmans had to change from the chaise to a stagecoach and spend several days along the way. Never had Laura been on such a long journey; never had she felt herself in the midst of so many strangers. She tried to hide behind her mother's skirts and her father's greatcoat. When would they get to wherever it was they were going?

After what must have seemed to Laura an endlessly long time the coach finally stopped. Mr. and Mrs. Bridgman and Laura were helped out. Laura clung to her mother as they went up a short flight of stairs and into a building. In an-

other moment Laura felt her small hand once again held by the large hand that belonged to the unusually tall man who had visited her once in Mill Village. Was this his home? What was she doing here? No one could explain, of course.

Then Laura felt a woman's soft hand take hers. Laura could not know that this was Miss Jeannette Howe. Laura and her mother took off their coats and bonnets. Following the strange woman they walked along — what was it? A room? A hall? Laura could somehow sense the largeness of the rooms. She was accustomed to small, low-ceilinged rooms at home. She felt very small and lost in so much space. She clung to the strange but friendly woman on one side of her and to her mother on the other.

Now they had entered a smaller room and she was allowed to feel about. There was a bed, a rocking chair, a washstand and a little table. The furnishings here were not unlike those in her own room at the farm. She was encouraged to help her mother take her dresses and other clothes out of the trunk in which they had been placed at home. Were they perhaps going to stay here for a visit? Where was her mother's bag?

There, now they had come to her box of treasures. She felt her mother take it and place it on the table by the bed. Was this going to be her own room? Would her little brothers, Addison and John, be coming too? Would her treasures be safe on the table? No one can know whether questions such as these passed through Laura's mind and no one, of course, could have made her understand the answers to them.

Now they were going back through the long hall to the large room from which they had come. Laura was led over to a low chair near her father and the tall man and given a cup of milk and a cookie. When she had finished eating she sat quietly in her chair.

Then she felt people getting up around her.

Her father leaned down and patted her. Laura started to jump up. That pat usually meant that he was going away. His firm hand pushed her back down into the chair again. Now her mother leaned over and patted her.

Laura was terrified. This too was a goodbye pat. Surely her father and mother were not going away! Surely they were not going to leave her in a strange place! Laura struggled to get out of the chair. But now it was the large hand of the friendly man and the gentle hand of the woman that were holding her back.

Laura felt a door close. She was allowed to get out of the chair and she rushed madly in the direction in which she knew the door lay. It was closed. Laura let out a loud unpleasant sound. It sounded almost like a wounded animal. She began crying and pounding on the door with her little fists.

"We must let her tire herself out some with her grief and tears," said Dr. Howe to his sister.

"She is already tired from the long journey, and the fear and sorrow of this separation will exhaust her further. In a little while we must take her to her room. Her box of treasures and her clothes at least will be familiar to her."

"Oh, Sam, it is so pathetic to see her frightened and upset," said Miss Jeannette. "If there were only some way to let her know that it is all for her own good that she has come here." Dr. Howe and his sister watched the terrified little girl crying, beating the door, feeling about the room for some familiar object or person. When she came near them they tried to comfort her, but each time she would draw away.

At last, when they felt that Laura would allow it, they led her to her room. They left her there and locked the door. When Miss Jeannette returned in less than half an hour she found Laura sound asleep on her bed.

"We can expect that there will be several more scenes like the one we have just witnessed before Laura will accept the fact that she must stay here," said Dr. Howe to his sister.

"Of course!" said Miss Jeannette. "Can you imagine how she must feel? Suddenly, with no warning — for how could anyone warn her? —

she has been taken from the familiar surroundings of the farm, separated from her father, her mother, her little brothers and her good friend Mr. Tenney. Why, it is as if she had been suddenly plunged into an even darker prison than the one she has always lived in: still no light, no sound, almost no smells or tastes and now not even the familiar things and people around her to touch!"

"I had thought of having Mrs. Bridgman remain here at the school for a few days," said Dr. Howe. "But I decided that since Laura is so bright and friendly, she would recover from the shock of separation quickly and I could begin her education sooner if we did not have to wean her gradually from her mother. I hope I am not wrong about this."

"She *is* bright and friendly, Sam," said Miss Jeannette enthusiastically. "I could see that even in the little while before her parents left."

And Dr. Howe was right in thinking that

Laura would quickly recover from the first shock of separation. In less than a week Laura began to be her own lively self once more. She began to reach out with her wonderful hands to learn all she could about her new home.

The room that had been given to Laura was in Dr. Howe's own apartment and he and his sister quickly became another father and mother to her. In a very short time she began learning, through her hands of course, to identify every member of the school family. There were more than forty people: blind children and teachers. Laura soon knew every one of them by touch.

At the end of two weeks Laura was so happy in her new surroundings that Dr. Howe felt he could begin the experiment he had planned. The night before he began he discussed his plans aloud with his sister.

"My goal is perfectly clear to me, Jeannette," he said. "I am going to try to bring into Laura's mind the idea that there are twenty-six different

signs or letters that everyone uses. This is our
alphabet. I want her to know that by combining

these letters into words we can share our thoughts with each other."

"But Sam, how in the world are you going to 'tell' Laura that?" asked Miss Jeannette, puzzled. "If she were just blind you could have her feel the raised-up letters with her fingers and tell her their names. Or, if she were just deaf and mute, you could show her letters. But she is blind and deaf and mute, so what can you do?"

"I know just exactly how I am going to try to do it," said Dr. Howe, smiling. "You may attend the first class with Laura tomorrow morning and see for yourself."

THE GREAT DAY dawned. When the first lesson began Laura was seated at a table across from Dr. Howe. Beside her sat Miss Drew, who was to be Laura's own special teacher. Miss Jeannette Howe sat watching nearby.

The doctor had arranged a row of objects on the table in front of him. There were a large key, a spoon, a knife, a fork, a book, a cup and a few other things with which he felt sure Laura would be familiar.

First Dr. Howe put the key into Laura's hand. It was a very large key. He let her handle it and feel it all over. She knew immediately what it was. The key at home with which she locked her boot in the cupboard was very much like this one — except for one thing. Her sensitive fingers paused as they felt the long key. There was something *on* this one.

Dr. Howe had fastened a paper label on the key. On the label the word *key* was written in a special kind of raised lettering or embossing that was used at that time in writing for the blind. The Braille system, now so widely used, had not yet been adopted. Dr. Howe guided Laura's fingers over the raised lines of the letters several times. She had no idea, of course, what the letters were.

Then he took the key away from Laura and handed her a spoon. She took it, felt it and immediately recognized it as a spoon much like the ones with which she set the table at home. Again there was one important difference. Along the handle of the spoon Dr. Howe had pasted a label with the letters S-P-O-O-N written in raised type. Dr. Howe guided her fingers carefully over this word several times.

Now the doctor took away the spoon and
gave the key back to Laura. He directed her
fingers to the label on the key again. Then he
gave her back the spoon and directed her fingers
to the label on the spoon once more. He wanted
Laura to feel that the shape of the lines on the
key label and the shape of the lines on the spoon
label were just as different from each other as
the key and spoon themselves were different
from one another.

Somewhere, thought Laura, I have felt lines
like these before, but where? Was it on my
plate that Uncle Asa gave me?

Now the doctor did something else. He took
away the key and the spoon and gave Laura
just a piece of paper with some raised letters on
it. The letters were K-E-Y again. Taking the
key once more, Dr. Howe directed Laura's
fingers to the label on it.

An expression on Laura's face made it quite
clear that she recognized that the raised letters

were the same on both papers, the one on the key and the separate label. Dr. Howe went through the same process with the spoon and a separate label that read S-P-O-O-N.

The rest of that first lesson was spent letting Laura feel the remaining objects — cup, knife, book, and so forth — and the labels for these, both those pasted on the object and those that were separate. From that time on Laura had lessons every morning and afternoon. She seemed to enjoy them thoroughly and to consider them just a game, not work. It was difficult for Dr. Howe and Miss Drew to get her to stop "playing" this game.

By about the third day Dr. Howe and Miss Drew were delighted to see that Laura had grasped the important point that the separate label for *key* somehow went with the key and the label that was separate from the spoon went with the spoon. That she understood this was shown by the fact that she could take a separate

label, such as the one spelling *book*, and feel
about until she found a book without any label.
Then she would place the label on the book.

In a very few days Laura could reverse this
process. She could pick up an object, such as a
spoon, search through a pile of loose labels on
the table, feel them until she found the one that
read S-P-O-O-N and then put it on a spoon.
She could do this for any object for which she
had been taught the feeling of the word.

Dr. Howe was greatly encouraged. He felt
sure that he was going to succeed with Laura;
his only question was how long it was going to
take him. In a report that he once wrote about
his work with her he said: "It sometimes
occurred to me that she was like a person alone
and helpless in a deep, dark, still pit, and that I
was letting down a cord and dangling it about,
in hopes she might find it, and that finally she
would seize it by chance, and, clinging to it, be

drawn up by it into the light of day and into human society."

The lessons were going so well that Dr. Howe felt Laura was ready to take another important step forward. He had Miss Drew cut the labels for the words *key*, *spoon*, *knife*, and so forth, into separate letters. Up until this time Laura had seen words as wholes. Now he wanted her to learn that they are made up of parts — letters. Laura was allowed to follow closely, with her hands, all that Miss Drew did. After the words had been cut into separate letters, her hands followed Miss Drew's as she arranged the letters back into words.

In an astonishingly short time Laura had grasped the point of this new "game." If Miss Drew handed her the letters O, S, N, O, P, in a flash Laura could arrange them in the correct order to spell S-P-O-O-N. If Miss Drew gave her Y, K, E, Laura arranged them into the word K-E-Y. O, K, O, B and I, K, E, N, F were

equally simple for her. After a few more lessons Laura could do this with all the words in her vocabulary and soon after that she could take from a whole pile of loose letters whatever ones she wanted and spell correctly any word she wished of those she had been taught. This would have been a great accomplishment for any eight-year-old. How much more remarkable it was for a little girl like Laura Bridgman!

Dr. Howe thought it would be easier for Laura to arrange the letters if there were some kind of form into which they could be fitted. Therefore he had metal letters — types, he called them — made for her and a frame with grooves into which the letters could be fitted. He had four complete sets made of the twenty-six letters of the alphabet. Within a short time Laura was using the metal letters to build all the words she knew.

Two months had passed before Dr. Howe felt that Laura was ready to take the final step that he had planned for her. Miss Drew was sent to the home of a Mr. George Loring, who was a deaf-mute, to learn the manual alphabet. She learned it in one afternoon.

The manual alphabet is a way of forming the twenty-six letters of the alphabet with the hands. In the United States the one-handed manual alphabet is used. There is also a two-handed system used in some countries. In the one-handed system the letter *a*, for example, is formed by folding the four fingers over and keeping the thumb straight. *B* is formed by holding the fingers straight up with the thumb folded in. In only a few cases, as with *c* and *y*, for example, does the hand form a shape that very much resembles the shape of that letter as we write it.

A deaf person who has been "talking" with the manual alphabet for a long time can "say" with his hand as many as 130 words a minute. A deaf person who is skilled at watching another person "speak" with his hands can easily "read" 130 words a minute.

Laura, of course, would not be able to see the letters. Miss Drew would have to form them in Laura's hand so that she could feel them.

But how could she teach Laura that the various positions in which she held her fingers meant the letters of the alphabet that she had already

learned with raised letters and metal types? This
is how Miss Drew did it. She picked up the key
and let Laura feel it. Then she took the letter K
from the set of metal types and let Laura feel
that. Then she shaped the letter *k* in the manual
alphabet into Laura's hand, her first two fingers
up and bent forward, the next two fingers folded
down, and the thumb up. She made Laura feel
the way her fingers were held. Then she let
Laura feel the metal letter K again.

The same procedure was followed with the
letter *e*. First Laura must feel the metal type of
the E, then Miss Drew formed *e* in the manual
alphabet, all the fingers folded over and the
thumb folded down, and then back to the metal
type again. Finally the letter Y was taken from
the metal types and Laura allowed to feel it. The
manual *y* is formed with thumb up, little finger
up and other fingers all folded down. This one
almost looks like a *y* as we write it. Now Miss
Drew had set the metal types K-E-Y in the form.

She let Laura run her hand over the whole word. Then she formed again, in the manual alphabet, the letters *k-e-y* in Laura's hand and she placed the key itself in Laura's other hand. This was done with the spoon, the cup, and the key again.

And then it happened! For two months Laura had been "playing" these games with

letters and words almost the way a trained dog performs certain tricks. Now, suddenly, it was different. Dr. Howe always said that he knew almost the exact moment when Laura's face showed that she at last really understood what all this meant. Suddenly it seemed to become clear to her that every object had a name, that these names could be spelled by letters, either in raised letters, metal types or, most easily of all, by the manual alphabet.

In one of his yearly reports about his work with Laura Bridgman, Dr. Howe wrote:

. . . Now the truth began to flash upon her, her intellect began to work, she perceived that here was a way by which she could herself make up a sign of anything that was in her own mind, and show it to another mind, and at once her countenance lighted up with a human expression . . . I could almost fix upon the moment when this truth dawned upon her mind and spread its light to her countenance. . . .

Laura had found the rope that Dr. Howe was dangling before her. She had caught hold of it at last and could be drawn up from the dark pit in which she lived into the light of day!

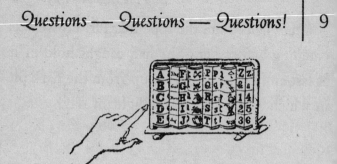

WHAT a different world it was for Laura now!

Can you imagine what it must have been like for her? She had been alive for eight years and yet until this day she had never been able really to ask a single question! Now, suddenly, she could ask at least one enormous question: WHAT IS THE NAME OF THAT?

Of course she didn't know the words *what*, *is*, *the*, *name*, *of*, and *that*, but now by placing her hand on any object, she let her teacher know that she was asking for the name of that object.

And ask she did! At supper on the day she really understood that every object has a name, poor Miss Drew didn't get a bite to eat. Laura wanted the name of everything and everybody. Usually at meals Miss Drew was expected to help not only Laura but several of the little blind girls. She cut their meat, buttered their bread and did anything else that needed doing. But tonight Laura demanded every single bit of Miss Drew's attention.

"I'll help with the other children," said Miss Jeannette. "This one meal we'll let Laura have you wholly to herself. It's a kind of birthday for her."

And so Laura began. She placed her hand on her napkin, and Miss Drew spelled "napkin" into Laura's hand. Then Laura spelled it into Miss Drew's hand. Then she asked the name of the tablecloth, the salt, the pepper, the sugar, the milk, and on and on and on. Miss Drew was thoroughly exhausted when she went to bed that night and the muscles of her spelling hand ached for hours.

Soon after her arrival at the school Laura had been given a real doll to play with. Now she taught the doll the manual alphabet. Of course Laura had to pretend that the doll had fingers that could move. She also taught the manual alphabet to many of the blind children so that they could talk with her.

When Laura had learned over one hundred common names of things her teacher decided that it was time for her to learn another kind of word. Words that tell the names of things are called nouns. Miss Drew felt that Laura was ready to learn action words, or verbs as they are called.

For her first lesson in verbs Miss Drew led Laura over to the door. She let Laura feel her shut it. Then she spelled "shut door" into Laura's hand. Laura already knew the word *door*. She wondered at first what a "shut" was.

Then Miss Drew opened the door. Then she spelled "open door" into Laura's hand.

It did not take Laura very long to understand that the words *shut* and *open* described what Miss Drew was doing to the door. Before the lesson was over Laura showed that she had understood perfectly. She went over to a window and opened it. Then she spelled "open window" in the manual alphabet. Then she shut the window and spelled "shut window." In this way Laura very quickly learned the most common verbs, like *open, shut, come, go, run, walk, sleep, eat,* and so on.

The next kind of words that Miss Drew taught Laura was what are called adjectives, words that tell us something about an object. Words like *soft, hard, smooth, rough, sharp* are all adjectives. Very soon Laura knew that among the treasures that she had brought from home was a *smooth* stone, a *sharp* porcupine quill, *soft* milkweed silk and a *spiral* snail shell.

There are many other kinds of words besides nouns, verbs, and adjectives that Laura needed to know in order to talk in sentences. There are words like *in*, *on* and *under* that are called prepositions; words like *soon*, *very* and *there*, which are adverbs; connecting words like *and*, *or* and *but*, and the little words *a*, *an* and *the*, which are called articles.

Some of these words were very difficult for Laura to learn because they were not names of

things, or things she could feel, or things her teacher could do. The only way for Laura to learn many of these words was to have other people use them and to use them herself.

Laura began making sentences simply by putting her words together in the order of what was most important to her. "Bread give Laura," was what she said when she wanted someone to give her a piece of bread. "Water drink Laura" of course meant that she wanted a drink of water, not that the water was going to drink her!

Every little child talks in this way at first. But as he listens to other people he gradually learns to put his words together in the way they do. But Laura could not hear people talking around her. If Miss Drew had had the time to "talk" into Laura's hand for many hours a day, Laura would have learned what we call grammar and sentence construction much more quickly. But Miss Drew did not have time to do this nor did she realize how important it was.

Laura did as well as she could, but her sentences never sounded just right. For example, in 1840 after one of her visits back to Hanover to see her family, she wrote: "When Laura did go to see mother, ride did make Laura side ache; horse was wrong, did not run softly."

It was not just the way we make our sentences that was a problem to Laura; the words themselves presented her with many difficulties also.

One day Miss Drew was teaching Laura the words *right* and *left*. To teach this she touched her own right hand and spelled "right hand" in the manual alphabet. She repeated this for her left hand, for both her feet, her ears and her eyes.

Bright little Laura understood it all. But then she had a question. She touched her own nose. She looked at her teacher with a puzzled expression. Which was her nose? Right? Or left? What could Miss Drew say? What would you have said?

Laura very soon experimented with making up words. One day when she did not feel like doing her lessons she told Miss Drew, "I feel very strongless." Miss Drew told her that there was no such word.

"But," said Laura, "when I do not sit still you tell me that I am restless. Why can I not say I am strongless when I do not feel strong?"

"That just isn't a word," explained Miss Drew patiently.

"All right then," said Laura, "I am very weakful!"

Poor Miss Drew had to explain that that was not a word either.

On another day Laura had been asked to take

a message to someone and to go *alone*. The teacher explained that *alone* meant "by herself." Laura did as she was told and returned.

A little while later she thought of somewhere else she wished to go. This time she wanted to take one of her blind friends with her.

"Laura will go al*two*," she said brightly. She had figured out that if al*one* meant by herself, al*two* meant with someone else.

She was very confused when a word that she already knew occurred as part of a longer word. One day after the school had moved to South Boston, which is near the ocean, she and Miss Drew were standing on the beach. The waves were crashing and Laura asked what made the sand shake under her feet.

"The waves are jarring the ground," said Miss Drew.

"Who put jar in the ground?" asked Laura.

In spite of such difficulties, Laura made wonderful progress and before long she was reading the books in raised type that were used by the blind students in the school. Reading presented her with new problems. For one thing, she would read along in a sentence and try to understand it word by word instead of reading the whole sentence to find the meaning.

In a book written by Dr. Howe for the blind children, part of one sentence bothered her every time she read it. The sentence was: "You must not think because you are blind that you can not learn as much as other children."

When Laura read it she would read: "You must not think because you are blind —" Here she would stop. With a worried look on her little face, spelling into Miss Drew's hand, she would ask, "Why did the doctor tell blind girls they must not think?"

Laura was soon ready to start arithmetic, and she did very well. But when she was old enough to do problems, she could not understand that the problems were not written especially for her

and that she was just supposed to do the arithmetic in them.

Once a problem was read to her: "If you can buy a barrel of cider for four dollars, how much can you buy for one dollar?"

After thinking a minute she asked, "How did the man who wrote the book know I was here?" And then she added, "I cannot give much for cider because it is very sour."

When Laura first started the study of geography it was naturally very difficult for her to imagine the tremendous size of our world or even of our country. The blind children were taught their geography on relief maps on which the mountains were raised above the level of the rivers and valleys so that they could feel them. An enormous globe over thirteen feet in diameter was also used.

Still Laura had a very difficult time grasping the distances involved. One day her teacher was giving her a lesson about Niagara Falls. She was describing the great height of the falls and the loud noise the water made as it crashed down on the rocks below.

"Can you hear them now?" Laura asked her teacher.

"Oh, no!" said Miss Drew. "They are much too far away."

"Be very quiet," said Laura. "Listen carefully. Now don't you hear them?"

As Laura learned to "talk" and to "hear" with her hands, she discovered more and more about herself as well as about everything else. Gradually she learned how different she was from other people. She was told that other people talked with their mouths, saw with their eyes, and heard with their ears.

Strangely enough, she did not seem upset that she could not do all of these things. When she asked Miss Drew one day what *voice* meant,

her teacher explained that voice is the noise
people make when they talk with their mouths.

Laura thought for a minute. "I do not voice,"
she said.

One thing about her many handicaps did
bother her, however. She did not like it one bit
when she learned that dogs, which she considered inferior to people, could hear when
people spoke with their mouths, but that she, a
person, could not. That did not seem right to
her.

As the years passed, Laura Bridgman studied
every subject that other children study and in
all of her subjects she showed a keen mind and
eager curiosity. Dr. Howe, Professor Mussey,
James Barrett, Asa Tenney, and her own mother
and father had all been right about Laura. She
was a very bright little girl.

Many of Laura's teachers kept careful records
during the years they spent working with her.
Here are a few of the questions that Laura asked

them. How many could you have answered if you had been the teacher?

"Who made water?"

"Why do not our hearts stop?"

"Why has fish not legs?"

"Why do not flies and horses go to bed?"

"Why does it rain?"

"Do *think, guess, suppose, understand* all mean the same?"

"Are there people in the sun?"

"Can flies go up to the sun?"

"How do we know there is air?"

"What is wind made of?"

"Why does a waterfall not stop?"

"Is God ever surprised?"

It WAS NOT long before the name of Laura Bridgman had become known all over the United States and parts of Europe. There were two reasons for this.

Dr. Howe, as director of the school, wrote each year a report of the progress of his work. He was so enthusiastic that what he wrote made exciting reading. It was even more exciting after he began his work with Laura Bridgman. Before many years had passed Dr. Howe's annual reports were as eagerly awaited as a fascinating new book.

Dr. Howe also began the practice of holding an open house at the school on the first Saturday of each month. He did this because he was eager to have people see for themselves how much his blind students could learn. When he had begun his work most people did not really believe that blind children could be educated.

And so on the first Saturday of each month the doors of the school were thrown open to anyone interested enough to walk in. Before long, hundreds of people were coming to these monthly "exhibits," as they were called. Here the public could see and hear blind children reading books printed in raised type. They could watch blind children work their arithmetic problems on special metal cases that had been developed for this purpose.

They could watch and listen as the children recited their geography lessons, tracing with their sensitive hands the mountains and rivers on the relief maps and huge globes that Dr. Howe had had made for them. Other students spun, wove, played on a variety of musical instruments

and did almost anything that seeing children
could do.

Dr. Howe felt sure that if the public, whose
tax money helped pay for this work, saw how
much the blind could do, they would be more
willing to give money for these purposes. He
also arranged at different times to take some of
the pupils before the state legislature, the men
who decide how taxes should be spent, so that
they too could know and care about the work
being done with the blind.

By 1839 Laura Bridgman had become one of
the main attractions at the exhibits. Thanks to
Dr. Howe's reports and the newspaper stories
that were written about these reports, thousands
of people began coming to the monthly exhibits
to see this remarkable little girl.

Indeed, before long, such crowds gathered
around Laura as she sat demonstrating her
sewing, or her skill in arithmetic, or her ability
to write with a regular paper and pencil, that

her teachers thought it best to surround her desk with benches. In this way a little enclosure was made that held back the crowd and kept them from pressing in too closely.

The first time this was done Laura did not like it. She thought it was done to keep her from harming the people, not the people from harming her. She asked: "Are the ladies afraid of me?"

In 1842, when Laura was thirteen years old, one of the most famous men in the world at that time came on a visit from England to America. His name was Charles Dickens. He was an author whose books are still read and loved. Some of his best-known works are: *David Copperfield*, *Oliver Twist*, and *A Christmas Carol*.

There was one person in the United States whom he wanted to be sure to see and that was Laura Bridgman. He had read Dr. Howe's

reports about Laura and he wanted to see this unusual child himself.

After his visit with her at the school he wrote about her in his book *American Notes*. Charles Dickens was one of the most widely read authors of his day so the name of Laura Bridgman became even more famous as a result of his story about her.

But there was another even more wonderful result. About forty years after Dickens made his visit, the mother of another little deaf, blind and mute girl in Alabama read his account. This woman's daughter, Helen Keller, was about six years old at the time. Like Laura Bridgman, Helen had become deaf and blind from a raging fever at about the age of two. Like Laura, because of an unusually bright and active mind, by the age of six, she was becoming much too difficult for her parents to control.

When Mrs. Keller read the story of Dr. Howe's successful educational experiment with Laura Bridgman in Dickens's *American Notes*, she suggested to her husband that they write to Perkins Institution for help. Dr. Alexander Graham Bell, the inventor of the telephone, who had been a teacher of the deaf for many years and who had seen little Helen Keller, also suggested that they turn to Perkins for help.

And so a teacher was chosen — Anne Mansfield Sullivan. In preparing herself for this difficult job Miss Sullivan spent long hours reading the records that Dr. Howe, Miss Drew and other teachers had kept of their work with Laura Bridgman. When Miss Sullivan left for

Alabama she took in her suitcase a doll that
Laura Bridgman, who was still living at Perkins
Institution, had dressed especially for Helen.
Two years later Miss Sullivan and Helen went to
Boston to visit Perkins, and Helen actually met
Laura Bridgman.

Ten years after Laura went to Perkins her
dear friend Asa Tenney died. She had returned
home for visits every year and had always spent
some time with Uncle Asa. For some reason, he
never let her teach him the manual alphabet.
Laura never forgot how much she owed to this
dear friend of her childhood. A few years after
his death she was asked to write a story about her
life before she was educated by Dr. Howe. In
the story she had a good deal to say about Asa
Tenney.

She wrote:

I had a small thin plate for my own, it was a gift from
an old man named Mr. Asa Tenney whom I always

loved. . . . The nice tin plate had the finger alphabet printed in raised letters around on the edge. . . . Mr. Tenney was always very patient and kind and gentle to me. [He] always dressed in most simple and frugal clothes . . . I derived a great pleasure from walking and rambling and sporting with Mr. T. daily. He used to go with me out of the doors in search of eggs very frequently. I liked so much to grope in hollowed nests with my little hands, seeking for a single egg.

. . . He influenced me with something like geography, which was, that I flinged sand, stones and gravels and branches of aged trees into the brook. I enjoyed that game extremely . . . He was stout and firm to lift me up in his big arms a long distance from place to place. I admired very much to be carried in his arms like a babe. We went out to pluck lots of different berries . . . Mr. T. never liked to scold me for doing a little thing which was really wrong according to his opinion. He never inflicted a punishment upon me in his life.

Laura Bridgman's other great friend, Dr.

Samuel Gridley Howe, died in 1876. She
realized how much she owed this great man,
also. After his death she wrote to a friend, "I
think of Dr. Howe day and night, with sorrow
and gratitude and love and sincerity."

For fifty-two years Laura Bridgman lived at
Perkins. Dr. Howe had arranged that she should
have a room at the school as long as she lived.
Through her sewing she was able to earn some
money and she was a real help in educating other
deaf, blind and mute children who came to the
school.

On the fiftieth anniversary of her coming to
Perkins Institute a great celebration was held
with Laura as the guest of honor. Dr. Howe's
wife, Julia Ward Howe, was in charge of the
party. Mrs. Howe had become very famous
herself because of the song she had written
during the Civil War, "The Battle Hymn of the
Republic." There was an enormous "birthday
cake," speeches were made by many famous

men, and parts of Dr. Howe's well-known reports were read. Two years later, at the age of sixty, Laura Bridgman died.

Dr. Howe once described the education of Laura Bridgman as a "sort of triumphal march." When we hear the words "triumphal march," most of us see a picture in our minds of a victorious army that has conquered a powerful enemy. We can almost hear them as they march past to stirring music with bright banners waving.

It seems strange to think of the education of a little deaf, blind and mute child as being anything like that. And yet, Laura Bridgman with the help of Dr. Howe, Dr. Mussey, James Barrett and Asa Tenney had conquered the enemies of darkness and silence. They had done it in the same way that a lighted candle conquers the darkness of the silent night.